Old BOWLING, DUNTOCHER, HARDGATE, MILTON and OLD KILPATRICK

by
John Hood

It was once, at certain times, possible to walk across the River Clyde at Old Kilpatrick. However, after the river was deepened in the 1700s, travellers had to be ferried across. Until the early years of the nineteenth century, the Old Kilpatrick ferry crossing was located at Ferrydyke, before it was moved half-a-mile up river to a site opposite Erskine. At that time, and until August 1904 when responsibility was transferred to the Clyde Navigation Trust, the crossing was privately run by Lord Blantyre and his heirs. From 1868 until the mid-1900s, when diesel-powered ferries were brought into service, ferries were typically steam-driven chain ferries similar to the one seen here. Although the four-minute crossing was generally uneventful, there were occasions when a variety of mechanical faults caused the ferry to be delayed or even grind to a halt. One such mishap occurred in early June 1964, when a fault in the hydraulic system prevented the landing ramps from functioning, leaving the ferry to shuttle backwards and forwards across the river for almost an hour. Presumably, the passengers were not amused!

ACKNOWLEDGEMENTS

I would like to thank the following people for their help: Graham Hopner and Mary Frances McGlynn (both West Dunbartonshire Libraries); Irene Galt, Edith Reid, Graham Rennie and Jimmy MacFarlane (all Bowling); Sam Gibson, Kathy Moore and Thomas Moore (all Hardgate); and Alex Brown, Nan Brown and Isabel Lees (all Old Kilpatrick). The publishers wish to thank the following for contributing photographs to this book: Alex Barr for the front cover, pages 1, 5–7, 9, 11, 12, 15 (left), 16, 18–20 (both), 21, 24, 28, 30, 35, 37, 38 (right), 39, 41, 43, 44, 45 (right), 46 and the back cover; Jack McGowan for the inside front cover and pages 2, 4, 8 (both), 10, 13, 15 (right), 17, 26 and 27 (left); Bill Smith for pages 23, 27 (right), 29, 31 and 36; and the author for pages 32–34, 40 and 47.

FURTHER READING

The books listed below were used by the author during his research. None of them are available from Stenlake Publishing. Those interested in finding out more are advised to contact their local bookshop or reference library.

Brotchie, A.W. and Grieves, R.L., *Dumbarton's Trams and Buses*, Dundee: N.B. Traction, 1985.

Bruce, John, *History of the Parish of West or Old Kilpatrick and of the church and certain lands in the parish of East or New Kilpatrick*, Glasgow: John Smith & Son, 1893.

Clydebank District Libraries, *Duntocher and Hardgate in pictures*, Clydebank: Clydebank District Libraries, 1983.

Clydebank District Libraries, *More Duntocher and Hardgate in pictures*, Clydebank: Clydebank District Libraries, 1984.

Clydebank District Libraries, *Old Kilpatrick in pictures*, Clydebank: Clydebank District Libraries, 1984.

McInnes, Angus, *The History of Old Kilpatrick*, Alexandria, Dumbarton: W. McKelvie, 1935.

The nineteenth century East Lodge on Bowling's Main Street was one of three lodges serving the Buchanan family's Auchentorlie Estate. The estate had been acquired by the Buchanan family in two stages over the years and comprised the lands of Littlemill, Dunglass, Dunnerbuck and Auchentorlie. The first lands (Littlemill and Dunglass) were purchased by Archibald Buchanan in 1812 and the second (those of Dunnerbuck and Auchentorlie) were purchased by him in 1827. All three lodges still remain today. Two (including East Lodge) stand on Main Street while the third is situated on Great Western Boulevard. Largely unchanged externally, East Lodge is now in private hands. Just visible to the left of the picture is one of two tenements built on the lands of Corsedelf. The earliest is Auchentorlie Terrace and dates from 1864, whilst the second dates from 1900.

INTRODUCTION

Until 1649, when it was divided into Old and New Kilpatrick, the villages of Bowling, Duntocher, Hardgate, Milton (more properly the 'mill town of Colquhoun') and Old Kilpatrick all formed part of Kilpatrick Parish. Thereafter, and for about 240 years, these five villages were part of Old or West Kilpatrick Parish. In 1889, the administration of the villages was transferred to the newly appointed Dunbarton County Council, and it remained so until 1975. At that time, Bowling and Milton became part of the new Dumbarton District Council and the other three became part of Clydebank District Council. In terms of their geographical situation, all five villages lie within an eight-mile long by five-mile wide strip of land, bounded on the north by the Kilpatrick Hills and, on the south, by the River Clyde.

Of the five, Old Kilpatrick is undeniably the oldest village. Its name, meaning 'church of Patrick', has led many to suggest that it is the birthplace of St Patrick, the patron saint of Ireland, however, this cannot be authenticated. What is certain, however, is that there was a Christian settlement there since medieval times. Unfortunately, the original church dating from that period was demolished in 1812 (and although described as being 'a very ancient edifice', the then parish minister, the Rev. William McCartney, categorically refused to preach in it because of its poor condition and instigated its demolition).

The principal landowners within the parish were the Colquhouns. Descended from one Humphrey de Kilpatrick, this family once held sway over most of the parish, with the exception only of lands gifted to Paisley Abbey in the twelfth century. Over a long number of years, however, the power of the Colquhouns declined and new families, such as the Buchanans of Auchentorlie and the Blantyre Stuarts, acquired vast local estates. This process continued into the nineteenth century, although by then it was wealthy industrialists like the shipbuilders, the Scotts of Bowling, or the cotton magnate William Dunn, whose successful business dealings enabled them to build up substantial properties throughout the parish.

Until the early 1700s, the predominant industry in the area had been farming. Thereafter Old Kilpatrick, along with Duntocher and Milton, briefly gained a number of small-scale industries. These were established on the banks of the several fast-flowing burns emanating from the Kilpatrick Hills. One of the earliest of these businesses was the Dalnotter Iron Works. This was first established on the lower reaches of the Lusset, or Dalnottar, Burn before later being re-established on the Duntocher Burn. The latter, being faster flowing, was ideal for industries such as corn mills, waulkmills, forges and nailworks which were located here. These industries were followed, firstly, by printing and bleaching works, and, later, cotton mills – which were also located on the Milton Burn. One of these was Milton Mill, established in 1787. This existed as a printing and bleaching works until 1871, when it was converted for the manufacture of paper.

Undoubtedly, however, the greatest concentration of industrial might was around the Duntocher Burn, for it was here, between 1808 and 1831, that four large cotton mills were set up. During this period, the establishment of these mills led to an increase in population and prosperity for Duntocher, Faifley and Hardgate. There were also improvements in road, canal and river travel. However, this prosperity was short-lived when, in the 1860s, the American Civil War brought about a collapse of the cotton trade. This led to closure of the mills and the villages of Duntocher and Milton in particular suffered a marked decline in population.

In contrast, Bowling, which had initially profited less from early industry and more from its situation on the picturesque Bowland Bay, steadily increased in importance throughout the nineteenth century. It benefited from its position at the western end of the Forth & Clyde Canal and from the opening, in 1850, of the first railway line on the north bank of the River Clyde. The canal was especially important to Bowling for, almost immediately, a small dry dock was built by entrepreneur, David McGill. The business dealt mainly with ship repairs and, by the 1830s, had flourished sufficiently to allow it to support two small shipyards. Some twenty years later, these two yards merged to form the shipbuilding firm of Messrs Scott & Sons (Bowling) Limited. The accessibility of good canal and rail links also provided the impetus to develop a well-equipped harbour at Bowling. This was used for the import and export of coal and metal ore. In addition, in 1916 a large oil depot was established at nearby Dunglass, bringing further prosperity to the area. Unlike the earlier printing works and cotton mills, these industries had longer lifespans. Even so, by the 1960s the industries in Bowling were in decline.

Today, there is little industry in this area and the residents of all five villages by and large tend to work in towns such as Clydebank and Dumbarton, or in Glasgow.

The power of the Milton Burn was first utilised in 1780 when the Colquhoun family erected a corn mill high up in Milton Glen. Seven years later, the mill and surrounding lands were acquired by Robert Millar (a local miller) in partnership with George and James Provand, for use as a bleaching and printing works. These works were sold to McDowall & Company in 1795, and their use changed to that of a cotton mill. In late 1833, while in the ownership of Patrick Muter, the mill workers downed tools in a dispute over equal wages. In the spring of the following year, with the dispute still unresolved, the owners brought in workers from Glasgow. Transported by river steamer, these workers were, for their own safety, accompanied by several companies of soldiers. Some of the soldiers were also quartered in the mill, to protect it from rioting by the striking workers. In the latter half of the 1800s, the mill's use changed yet again – this time to the production of paper. It was acquired by the Glasgow firm of John Collins around 1879 and finally closed down around 1917.

These houses on Milton Brae were built by the proprietors of nearby Milton Mill to house their workers. Located high above the steep-sided Milton Glen, the houses were among the first to be built in Milton. Because of their elevated position, a strong stone dyke (seen here to the right of picture) was built on one side of the road – this presumably acted both as a retaining wall and also as a safety barrier for people using the road! Seen here, within the original older properties, is Jeannie Neil's general store, which at one time was the only shop in Milton. As late as the 1930s, the houses were still illuminated by paraffin lamps and lacked a regular supply of water, this having to be drawn from local wells. Whilst in the ownership of the Buchanans of Auchentorlie, the houses were ultimately condemned as uninhabitable and were subsequently demolished. In mid-1964, the present day Miltonhill estate was completed on the site. Designed by J.E.C. Campbell, the 29 houses on the estate were a mixture of terrace and Scandinavian-style red cedar houses. This new estate, said at the time to be the first of its kind in Scotland, gave its tenants sole responsibility for their own properties.

The now derelict Dunglass Castle was built as a stronghold around 1380 by Sir John Colquhoun. Over a hundred years later, in 1489, it was used by James IV during his siege of nearby Dumbarton Castle. Dunglass Castle was finally left in ruins by Oliver Cromwell in the mid-1600s, during his subjugation of Scotland. The castle walls can be seen here, surrounding the nineteenth century Dunglass House. This house was, for a period, the home of artist Talwin Morris – a friend of the architect, Charles Rennie Mackintosh. A tall obelisk was erected in 1838 on a rocky promontory behind the castle in memory of Henry Bell, the builder of the *Comet* – Europe's first passenger river steamer. In 1912, on the 100th anniversary of the *Comet*, the obelisk was decorated with evergreen shrubs and the inhabitants of nearby Bowling were asked to keep their house lights on in the evenings to create a 'spectacle'! Although traditionally there had always been a recognised right of way to Dunglass Castle, when Esso opened their oil depot there in 1916, access to the castle was prohibited. This was fiercely resisted by Bowling residents and was a local *cause célèbre* for many years.

The once separate village of Littlemill derived its name from the Little Mill of Auchentorlie which stood on a site later occupied by Messrs Hay, Fairman & Company's Littlemill Distillery. This operated from 1770 until 1985 and some of its buildings can be seen here, beyond the single-storey cottages. The cottages in the photograph, which date from 1781, stood at the junction of Main Street and Littlemill Lane, and were known locally as Tile Row because of their red tiled roofs. At different times over the years parts of the row were used by, amongst others, the local smiddy, the village school and Sinclair's grocery. From 1837 until 1872 Dunglass Post Office was also located here. The district's first post office, its demise came a few years after a post office was opened in nearby Bowling. Tile Row was demolished in 1900 and today the site forms part of the Littlemill Inn car park. Seen here to the rear of Tile Row is Findlay Cottage, a private dwelling once owned by the Scott family of shipbuilding fame.

This photograph shows the black-and-white mock-Tudor-style Horse Shoe Bar – now re-named Littlemill Inn. Standing on Main Street, it once marked the boundary between the villages of Littlemill and Bowling. It stands on the site of the once-celebrated Dunter's public house, a venue much frequented in the 1800s by Glaswegians drawn to Bowling when the village was renowned as a health resort. The high wall to the left of the picture marks the entrance to Littlemill Lane. On the ground behind the wall at one time stood the local shipyard's works canteen. Prior to 1970, when this area became part of a car park for the Littlemill Inn, it was occupied by a bus garage. On Paterson's Land (in Littlemill Lane) are several cottages dating from the 1790s. These used to be known locally as Chisel Row, because several were occupied by local joiners. Around 1987 the cottages were purchased from the Littlemill Distillery Company Limited by local tradesman, Jimmy MacFarlane, who extensively renovated them. Beyond the Horse Shoe Bar can be seen Park House, built by Robert Scott in 1893.

Directly opposite East Lodge is the former Bowling Public School and Hall. Dating from 1861, it was erected by public subscription to replace the school in Tile Row. In 1872, the building was handed over to the newly elected Old Kilpatrick School Board. It closed fifteen years later, when the new Board School was opened in Old Kilpatrick. Thereafter, almost seven years of wrangling ensued between the board and two competing sets of trustees before the building was finally gifted to the community for use as a public hall. In 1906, responsibility for the hall was transferred to the Landward Committee of the Parish Council. Although nowadays somewhat changed in appearance, it still functions as a public hall. All the properties seen here to the east of the hall (including the three-storey tenement at Woodside Place) have now gone. This tenement, which was demolished in 1980, was at one time known by locals as 'Ham and Egg' Place, due to the aroma from Sunday breakfasts being cooked by the railway workers who occupied the houses!

Between 1896 and 1951, Bowling was served by not one, but two, railway lines! The earliest of these was nine miles long and ran between Balloch and Bowling. Opened on 15 July 1850, it allowed travellers to Glasgow to go by rail to Bowling, where they transferred to river steamer to complete the rest of their journey. At that time, the eighteenth-century Frisky Hall (which stood near the station) was converted into a hotel to cater for the travellers. The hotel's importance diminished, however, when the railway line was eventually extended to Glasgow in 1858. The second line was the Caledonian Railway Company's Lanarkshire & Dunbartonshire line. This was opened on 1 October 1896 and ran between Glasgow and Dumbarton. The construction of the Bowling to Dumbarton and Bowling to Old Kilpatrick sections was undertaken by Sir Robert McAlpine and necessitated the blasting of a short cutting through the local Auchentorlie estate. On 5 February 1951, passenger services on this second line were withdrawn and today all that can be seen is the railway platform and the now boarded-up entrance hall to the rear of Scott Avenue.

The construction of Bowling Lower Harbour between 1846 and 1850 was undertaken jointly by the Balloch & Dumbarton Railway Company and Clyde Trustees. Shortly afterward, in September 1851, Clyde Trustees installed a mooring station to enable river steamers to lie over in the Lower Harbour during the winter months. Thereafter, until 1953 when alternative anchorage was built further down river, the harbour served as the winter quarters for the river steamers. It is said that locals used to be able to tell when summer had arrived – simply by the disappearance of the steamers from the harbour! It was also used by river steamers temporarily taken out of service, or 'mothballed' prior to scrapping. One such steamer was the *Marchioness of Lorne*, which was berthed in the harbour for a year before being taken to Dumbarton for scrapping. In addition, the harbour provided a sheltered mooring for small craft, such as Messrs Scott & Sons' steam yacht *Carola*, seen here to the right of the picture.

Although also used as winter quarters for river steamers, Bowling Harbour's primary function was as a port for the import and export of raw materials such as coal and pig iron. In the early 1900s, for example, an average of approximately 6,500 tons of coal was being exported each year. To deal with the ever-increasing tonnages being handled, the harbour and facilities were constantly upgraded. In 1907, the main wall of the harbour was rebuilt to enable new cranes to be installed, thus allowing dockers to simultaneously unload two large steamers instead of just one. Nine years later, the harbour facilities were further enhanced when the old steam cranes were replaced with new electric ones. Typically, for discharging purposes, the empty wagons would be shunted from the main railway line into a siding at the harbour, whereupon Clydesdale horses would pull the wagons under the electric cranes for loading. Thereafter, the Clydesdales would pull the loaded wagons back into the sidings to be made up again into trains.

The Gothic-style Bowling United Free Church, seen here opposite Sommerville Terrace, was designed by Glasgow architect James Marshall and opened in December 1869. Initially, it was built as a mission station of the Barclay United Free Church in Old Kilpatrick, but in 1877 its congregation succeeded in having the church declared an independent charge. On 4 March 1908, the Bowling Church amalgamated with the Bankside United Free Church in Old Kilpatrick – the former having a congregation but no minister, and the latter a minister but no congregation! Next to the church can be seen the white-painted wooden Columbia Cottage. Around 1870, this was shipped across to Scotland from Vancouver in Canada by local shipmaster, Captain James Scott. Next again is the former Buchanan Institute Reading and Recreation Rooms, which were opened in December 1884. Designed by John Paton, an Old Kilpatrick man, they were gifted to the citizens of Bowling by Captain R.D. Buchanan of Auchentorlie. Although members normally paid an annual subscription, short stay residents, such as sailors in port for a week or two, were given free access to the institute.

In this view of Bowling Main Street, taken at the turn of the twentieth century, the properties on Windsor Place, Allan's Land and Anderson Place can be seen to the right of the picture. The first of these, Windsor Place, was a three-storey tenement built by David Reddie, a local businessman who was also responsible for the conversion of shipmaster William Findlay's house into the Railway Restaurant (now the Railway Inn). During the Clydebank Blitz of March 1941, the portion of Windsor Place nearest the camera (including the single-storey annexe housing the Medical Hall) was badly damaged and had to be demolished. After lying derelict for several years, a block of six four-apartment houses was built on the site of the blitzed houses in the late 1940s. Since this photograph was taken, all of the houses west of Windsor Place have been replaced with new housing. On the opposite side of Main Street, the tenements on the extreme left of the picture have likewise been demolished.

In this 1930s view of Main Street, we can see Windsor Place and all of the properties on the south side of Main Street as far east as Red Row. Among the early businesses in Windsor Place were Leo Moscardine's restaurant and ice cream parlour, Thomas Palmer's bakery and, from 1932, Bowling Post Office. Beyond Moscardine's is the entrance to Manse Brae (at the stone wall which juts out). Manse Brae once acted as the boundary between the lands of East and West Dyke and, until 1858, was little more than a farm track. In that year, however, the surrounding land was freed up for building purposes and several substantial properties were then built. Amongst these were Craiglee Villa (the residence of the Rev. D.D. Robertson of Bowling United Free Church) and Strathclyde (from 1886 until 1891, the residence of shipping magnate, Sir William Burrell, of Burrell Collection fame). On the opposite side of Main Street, all but the Bay Inn, Craigview and the Red Row tenement have been demolished.

This early view of Main Street, taken near the entrance to Manse Brae, shows all the properties east of Saughfield House. Firstly, on the extreme right, is Saughfield House, where Bowling Post Office was located from 1868 until 1932. This and the adjoining property have now been demolished and there is currently a gap site here. The third property from the right is the Bay Inn. This was built in 1826 and is largely unchanged externally. The next property is Craigview, in which was located the Bowling branch of Dumbarton Equitable Co-operative Society. This building has also survived, but the Co-operative premises have now been converted into a private dwelling house. Beyond Craigview is a red-brick tenement, perhaps not surprisingly known as Red Row. This property dates from 1894 and was built by Lord Blantyre. East of Red Row is the former Lanarkshire & Dunbartonshire bridge. This used to carry the railway line over Main Street, but is now part of a walkway and cycle path.

Copyright

Sutherland Terrace, Bowling.

Sutherland Terrace, situated on Main Street at the eastern end of Bowling, was built in 1906 by the Misses Freebairn, daughters of a local spirit dealer. Although primarily comprising 'room and kitchen' accommodation, it was also at one time the location of Bowling Police Station. However, in May 1958 the station was closed and the village policeman transferred to Old Kilpatrick. Immediately to the east of Sutherland Terrace, was the site of the once popular Sutherland Arms Hotel. Formerly known as the Bowling Inn, it was purchased in 1845 by Charles Stuart, twelfth Lord Blantyre. He renamed it in honour of his wife, Lady Ann Evelyn Sutherland Gower, second daughter of the Duke of Sutherland. Reputedly, among its many visitors were Sir Thomas Lipton, the tea merchant, and the actress Ellen Terry. The hotel was demolished in 1925. Opposite the Sutherland Arms stood the old Bowling Toll Bar. This site is now Glen Park, once a popular venue for day-trippers and, since 1963, the location of Bowling's War Memorial.

At one time, Bowling residents would boast that their village stood at the 'highways of the world', for here road, rail, canal and river traffic all came together. Certainly, in this photograph all four are shown! On the extreme left, alongside the old turnpike road (now the A814 Dumbarton to Glasgow road), is the former London & North Eastern Railway line. Almost in the centre of the picture is the Forth & Clyde Canal. This was opened on 28 July 1790, when a hogshead of water from the River Forth was poured into the River Clyde at Bowling. Although the canal was closed on 1 January 1963, it has since been reopened. Crossing the canal is the former Caledonian Railway line, and finally, on the extreme right, is the River Clyde. Also in this photograph can be seen lines of railway wagons on the foreshore, formed up prior to being shunted alongside the canal basin and the harbour. This area was known locally as Bowling Lido.

THE LOCKS, BOWLING

Prior to 1990, when the Upper Canal Basin at Bowling was extensively refurbished by the British Waterways Board, it was not uncommon to see house boats tied up here. Some boat owners even made the canal basin their semi-permanent home and their children attended local schools. At the entrance to the Upper Basin was a double set of locks. These were opened and closed manually by the lock keeper, who lived in Helenslea – the house almost in the centre of this picture. As the water level of the canal was higher than the canal basin, the double set of locks had to be opened and shut in sequence to enable vessels to enter the canal basin. For many years, wooden logs destined for Temple Sawmills in Glasgow were brought into the basin, tied together to form rafts, then towed by horses up the canal to the sawmills. The ruins of the stables used for the horses can still be seen a few miles to the east, at Ferrydyke in Old Kilpatrick.

This view shows the wooden bascule bridge raised, and the railway bridge swung open, to allow a scow to proceed from the Upper to the Lower Canal Basin. The bascule bridge, which is still in use today, gave drivers and pedestrians access to both the banks of the Lower Basin and to Bowling foreshore. The railway bridge (now immobile and minus its lofty signal box) was built in the mid-1890s by Robert McAlpine. Unusually for the time, the bridge supports were constructed of concrete – rather than masonry or brick – using a method of construction perfected by McAlpine. Until 1931, when it was upgraded for electrical operation, the bridge was operated by steam power. Just visible behind the signal box is the roof of the nineteenth-century Custom House, which was also known as the Collector's House. Within the basin itself a coal staith, or chute, was erected in March 1901 to help load coal onto the little puffers, which would then transport it to west coast island communities. The coal trade ceased with the closure of the canal and the staith lay derelict until 1965, when it was finally demolished.

The former Gavinburn School (seen here from the playground to the rear of the school) was built by the Old Kilpatrick School Board to accommodate pupils from Old Kilpatrick and Bowling. Opened on 8 August 1887 by Board Chairman, James R. Thomson, it was substantially upgraded in August 1905, when various remedial measures were carried out and extra classrooms added. During the Blitz of March 1941, the school was badly damaged and only the headmaster's house (to the right of the picture) and the Infants' Department (left of the picture) were left standing. From then until 1954, when a new school was opened, most pupils were taught in temporary hutted accommodation on the site. In the 1930s, school dinners were known as 'five penny horrors'; apparently, while meat and stew dishes were popular, and rice, raisins and fruit preferred as desserts, soup and puddings were universally disliked. In June 1953, a later generation of pupils assembled in the playground where they each received a commemorative Coronation Day mug filled with sweets.

Between 1904 and 1905, three red-sandstone tenements were built on a wooded glen immediately to the west of the Parish Church Lodge. Situated between the Forth & Clyde Canal and Main Street, they were built in the shape of a hollow 'E'. This photograph shows the tenements, known as Gavinburn Terrace, shortly after completion. Although the development was generally welcomed, many locals regretted the loss of trees from the glen. Primarily residential, Gavinburn Terrace also had provision at each corner for commercial premises. For many years (and until 1941 when a local painter and decorator, James Gray, moved in) the near corner premises in this view were occupied by the Clydesdale Bank. Currently this unit is occupied by a financial advisor's office. The dairy shown alongside the bank has now been converted into housing. In the open fields immediately west of the terrace is the site of the most westerly fort on the Antonine Wall. Houses were built on this site between 1924 and 1925 under a State Assisted Scheme, and it was not unknown for residents to dig up the odd Roman coin! Today, these houses, in Gavinburn Gardens, remain largely unchanged.

Until 1855, Old Kilpatrick's drinking water came from local wells. One of these was St Patrick's Well (known locally as the Trees Well). Situated at the eastern corner of Gavinburn Terrace, it was closed in 1893 by Lord Blantyre (the feudal superior) due to fear of contamination. In 1931, the local Ratepayers' Association suggested that the well be reopened in the hope that its reputed association with St Patrick might attract visitors and consequently benefit local traders. Although samples taken at the time showed the water to be impure, it was agreed to reopen the well, provided the public were prevented from drinking its water. Accordingly, when it was reopened on 9 July 1932 by Lady Helen Baird (wife of Major William Baird, the then feudal superior), it had a lockable metal fence surrounding it. In April 1948, the trees beside the well (hence Trees Well) were removed, as their condition was giving rise to concern. When Main Street was realigned in 1951, the well was covered over. The area was then landscaped and a new drinking fountain installed, which was officially 'opened' on 9 March of the following year.

In this 1920s view of the junction of Main Street and Gavinburn Place, the Gavinburn Terrace tenement is on the right of the picture. On the left side of the road are the properties known as Kirkton. These consisted of three two-storey buildings which were erected in the late 1800s by the twelfth Lord Blantyre. Although well equipped for their time, the houses lacked any facility for washing household items. Residents were, however, provided with a communal wash house – a red brick building, which lay on the opposite side of Main Street, at the entrance to Sawmill Lane. The wash house was demolished in 1966, when the Kirkton houses were being pulled down to make way for new housing. Adjacent to the wash house (and just in picture beyond the coal cart) stood the Lodge of the Parish Church. More popularly known as the Round, or Inkpot, House because of its shape, this was demolished in 1931, along with the old church manse. The site later marked the entrance to Freddie Laing's nursery. Tramlines can be seen on the right-hand side of the road, parallel to the pavement.

In comparison to the previous photograph, this 1950s view of Main Street shows it without the tramlines. In addition, the fish and chip shop at the corner of Gavinburn Terrace has been replaced by the General Stores. This shop was opened in 1939 by Mrs Margaret MacMillan. Six years later, when her husband William retired from the railways, he went into partnership with her, although he concentrated mainly on the newsagent side of the business. After the MacMillans, the business was run by Mr Fry. Currently, it operates as a convenience store. To the left of the picture, beyond Kirkton, is the Old Kilpatrick Parish Church. This was the 'mother' church for the parish and although it only dates from 1812, it is in fact the third church to occupy this site since medieval times. In the far distance on Whisky Hill (so called because of the number of publicans who once stayed there) can be seen some of the Mount Pleasant villas, which were erected around 1906.

This photograph, taken around 1908, shows some of the older properties on Main Street from Old Church Place (to the right of the picture) to the Gushat Cross. Almost completely hidden behind Old Church Place is the red-sandstone tenement, New Church Place (just visible above the roof top). On the north side of Main Street can be seen Kirkton Dairy, Honey Cottage, Thistle Cottage, Clover Cottage, Comrie's Land, Tollbooth, Kay's Land and Clydeview. Running up the middle of Main Street is the Dumbarton Burgh & County tramline which ran between Dalmuir and Balloch. Also in the photograph is one of the passing loops which was built into this eleven-mile track. This particular loop ran from Main Street, through the centre of Old Kilpatrick, and on to Powside.

This further photograph of Main Street, looking east from Clover Cottage, can be dated from sometime between 1908 and 1928. In centre of picture is one of Dumbarton Burgh & County's trams, which first reached Old Kilpatrick on 25 June 1908. The public service commenced in the afternoon of that day and it is said that by early evening top side seats were hard to find. Certainly the tram shown here appears to be filled to capacity – and there appears to be a crowd of people waiting to board! Over the years, some of the long-established businesses on this part of Main Street included James Fleming (grocer), Strang (optician) and Mrs Wilhelmina Picken (outfitter). On Smith's Land, there was Margaret Graham's fruit and vegetable shop and the premises of licensed grocer, Robert McNair. At one time, Smith's Land was owned by local businessman Thomas Comrie. It is reported that, on his death in February 1902, all the village shops were closed as his cortege passed by as a mark of respect. All the properties seen here (both on and around Smith's Land) survived virtually unchanged until the early 1960s, when compulsory purchase resulted in their demolition. Shortly afterwards, a new shopping centre was built here.

This view of Main Street, looking west, was taken in 1947 from the entrance to Erskine View. This housing scheme was built between 1927 and 1928 under the auspices of the County Slum Clearing Scheme for the Improvement of Insanitary Areas. To the left of the picture, beyond Erskine View, is Crichton's Land and William Pirie's chemist shop. Beyond this, on New Church Place, can be seen the upper portion of Hogg's Building, which was erected around 1907. Within this was Hogg's Ettrick Bar, plus a butcher shop and a dairy. In 1970, Hogg's Building was demolished and today a rebuilt Ettrick Bar stands in its place. Almost directly opposite the entrance to Erskine View, on the north side of Main Street, is Tollbooth, which stands on Blantyre's Land. This two-storey property was built around 1855 by Lord Blantyre and replaced three earlier tenements which were known locally as the Tollbooth Buildings, because the old Tollbooth, or jail, had been situated here. Prior to the jail's demolition, it was a private house. Reputedly, its last occupant, Robert Donald, was better known to locals as 'Rab o' the jail'!

The introduction of the tram service to Old Kilpatrick necessitated the widening of Main Street and, consequently, many properties seen here had to be demolished. It is reputed that, on the day tram operations commenced, workmen were still busy clearing away rubble from the demolished properties! Amongst those affected on the south side of Main Street were the buildings from (but not including) the post office to New Church Place. Formerly, the post office had actually been situated on the opposite side of the street, within the three-storied Post Office Building. However in 1902, whilst Christina Tennant was Postmistress, the post office relocated across Main Street to occupy the old Parochial Board offices, as shown here. Since then it has undergone two further relocations: once in 1922, when it moved into ground-floor premises within the nearby Free Church Building; and again in 1932, when it moved to its present location in Erskine Place.

Street, Old Kilpatrick.

With the removal of the older properties around the Cross and the street-widening, Main Street was left with a decidedly more open aspect. When the post office relocated to the Free Church Building, its premises were then occupied by Archie Paul's newsagent and tobacconist (seen here to the left of the picture). By the early 1950s, the business was owned by Davie Graham. When the property was demolished in December 1966, Davie was rehoused in a new purpose-built shop on the opposite side of Main Street. On extreme right of picture is Clydeview (formerly known as the Post Office Building) and, on its left, Mac's Wine and Spirit vaults. The latter was run for many years by Miss Catherine (or Kate) MacArthur and was one of several long-established public houses in Old Kilpatrick. Others included William 'Pinkie' McLintock's Salmon bar, Duncan McIntyre's (situated opposite Kate's), John Anderson's Red Lion (at New Church Buildings), and another (with a sign sporting a bust of Sir William Wallace!) opposite the Tollbooth. Sandwiched between Mac's vaults and Tollbooth are the older properties on Kay's Land.

By 1957, when this view was taken, the area around the Cross had undergone further changes. Of these, the one making most impact was the demolition of the older properties on Kay's Land. These buildings were demolished in February 1931, after being condemned as uninhabitable. The site was then screened off with a high stone wall and more or less left derelict until the early 1960s. On the left, beyond Erskine View, is William Pirie's chemist shop. This business had first been established at Powside in 1913 by William's father, Robert. On the extreme right is Clydeview, housing John Smith's bakery – previously the bakery had been owned for many years by John Craig. Also trading from Clydeview over the years were Tausney's bicycle shop and Bill Butler's popular Old Kilpatrick Café. In the early 1960s, wholesale redevelopment of this area wiped out most of the properties seen here. Today, new housing, a public house and a small shopping centre have replaced them.

In 1858, when the Kilpatrick Upper Station was opened on the new Glasgow, Dumbarton & Helensburgh Railway line, the old turnpike highway to Duntocher (then known as Duntocher Road) was renamed Station Road. The highway had been constructed in the late 1770s and was controlled by a toll house, situated further down Duntocher Road (and out of picture). It was a single-storey, whitewashed building with a slated roof. The house, known as Toll Cottage, was extensively altered in 1896, but still survives today. However, the toll gates, which were adjacent to the toll house, were removed after the tolls were abolished on 1 June 1883. To the left of picture is Hillview Terrace and, in the distance, beside High Lusset playing fields, is the Old Kilpatrick Bowling Club pavilion. To the right of the picture can be seen the B-listed Lusset House, which was built by D.C. Paton in 1868 for Samuel Leckie, a Clydebank publican.

In this 1920s view, the Free Church Building (then housing the Post Office) is on the extreme left of the picture. Also known as Struther's Building, from about 1900 until 1922 the ground floor of these premises was occupied by James C. Struther's grocer's shop. After the post office relocated in 1932, the premises were used as a store by painter and decorator James Gray. The single-storey cottages beyond, on McDougall's Land, at one time housed Donald Wilkinson's smiddy, which was reputedly known as the 'rendezvous of idle frequenters'! The cottages were eventually condemned as uninhabitable and pulled down in October 1932. At that time, a new smiddy was built behind Mitchell Terrace (the tenement on the opposite side of the road, lying alongside Nellie Barr's Ashlea Cottage). After the cottages were demolished, local merchant William Armstrong erected Lilyoak on the site. This two-storey property contained a hardware and newsagent shop on the ground floor, with a house above. There was also a petrol pump alongside the shop and a garage to the rear. An agent for Morris cars, William was credited with selling the first Morris Tourer in Old Kilpatrick. The business was later taken over by William's daughter, Jean, and her husband, Duncan McGregor.

In this early view of Main Street, a No. 8 Dumbarton Burgh & County tram is seen approaching the passing loop at Powside, *en route* to Balloch. The Powside tenements (to the left of the picture) were built by Alexander McNee between 1905 and 1906, and contained flatted accommodation made up of either a 'room and kitchen' or 'two rooms and a kitchen'. At the time these flats were considered to be of 'superior class' as they had hot and cold water facilities! When first built, the ground-floor suite of shops was tenanted by Dumbarton Equitable Co-operative Society. The shops included fishmonger, butcher, draper and shoe departments. The fishmonger department also sold fruit and was especially popular with local children, who would buy penny bags of chipped fruit here. An added bonus was being able to feast their eyes on the beautifully decorated tiled walls showing, amongst other things, pastoral scenes and, of course, fish! Alongside the tenements can be glimpsed the former Old Kilpatrick gasworks manager's house. On extreme right of the picture is the single-storey Burnside Cottage at Burnside Place and, beyond, Glen View Terrace. In the main the buildings seen here have survived, however, new housing now occupies the gasworks site.

Until 1905, most of the land shown here was owned by the Scott family. Known as Bankside, the ground extended from Main Street to the canal. Today, with two exceptions, the properties in the photograph have all been demolished (including the two-storey building on the canal bank). The latter, known locally as the Granary, was built in the eighteenth century by the Scott family to store grain. It was eventually condemned, and demolished in August 1934. Still standing is the former Secession Church (to the right of the picture, partly visible to the rear of the stone wall) and Powside – seen beyond the gasworks chimney. Owned by the Dalmuir, Kilpatrick & Bowling Gas Light Company, the gasworks comprised eight retorts, producing 50,000 cubic feet of gas per day, and a gasometer of 25,000 cubic feet capacity. In 1891, the gasworks were taken over by the Partick, Hillhead & Maryhill Gas Company. They were closed in 1901. Of the towpaths, only one remains – that on the right-hand side of the picture.

CANAL . OLD KILPTRICK .

This early view of the canal was taken slightly to the east of Ferry Road. On the left can be seen Canal House and, on the right, the old Barclay United Free Church on Main Street. In the distance, on the north bank, is Storegate and, beyond, the Old Kilpatrick gasworks. Dalnottar Bridge in the centre of the picture was one of the many wooden bascule bridges which were erected on the Canal when it was first opened. With a heavy increase in cross river traffic, the bridge was eventually deemed inadequate. Consequently, it was replaced with a metal swing bridge, which was formally opened on 18 September 1934 by J.R. Rutherford, Convenor of Dunbarton County Council Highways Committee. The new bridge was designed by Glasgow engineers, Messrs Crouch & Hogg, and built by Messrs Sir William Arrol. Costing approximately £10,000, it consisted of a twenty-feet-wide roadway and two footpaths, each five feet wide.

In this 1957 scene, looking west from Ferry Road, the Dalnottar Terrace tenements can be seen on higher ground behind the old brick-built public toilets on Main Street. Built by Lord Blantyre in 1892, the terrace (outwardly at least) is little changed today. Further to the west beyond the war memorial is Storegate, where three houses originally stood. Among the oldest in Old Kilpatrick, one housed Duncan McColl's Ship Tavern, which was much frequented by cattle drovers bringing their herds across the River Clyde at Old Kilpatrick on their way to the market in Stirling. Two of the houses were demolished in late 1933, and the remaining property (which included Tommy Kempton's long-established Glen Lusset Bar) in February 1968. Just visible behind Storegate is the red-sandstone tenement at Glenend, which was demolished in 1966. On the opposite side of Main Street, at the entrance to Lusset Glen, is Erskine Place. Alongside this is the Blantyre Mission Hall, built and endowed by the twelfth Lord Blantyre in memory of his son, the Master of Blantyre.

At the end of the First World War, a committee was formed to facilitate the construction of a suitable memorial to commemorate the forty-nine local men who lost their lives during the war. Initially, it was proposed to site the memorial on vacant ground on Main Street. However, as the cost of this site was prohibitive, the committee gratefully accepted the offer by the feudal superior, Major William A. Baird, of a free site in front of Dalnottar Terrace. Designed by Glasgow architect P. MacGregor Chalmers and paid for by public subscription, the seventeen-feet-high memorial was unveiled by H.M. Napier of Milton on 10 September 1921. Although villagers were generally satisfied with the memorial, there were some who felt that a large glacial stone, known locally as 'the Big Boiler', should have been incorporated into it. This stone had lain for many years in a dyke at Dalnottar and was eventually used in the war memorial at Milton. In 1948, following road widening operations, the memorial was relocated to its present site at Storegate.

On 20 June 1843, in protest against the manner in which ministers were appointed (a Scotland-wide protest known as the Disruption), the Rev. Matthew Barclay of Old Kilpatrick Parish Church left the established church and, together with some of his congregation, established the Old Kilpatrick Free Church. Initially, the congregation worshipped in a marquee erected beside the local gasworks, until their new church was opened in June 1844. Built in Gothic style, the church was situated on Main Street, at the foot of Barclay Street. In addition, a manse was erected on higher ground to the rear of the church. Following the death of Matthew Barclay in 1865, the name of the church was changed to the Barclay Free Church. In 1866, the Rev. George McAulay was inducted as minister in succession to Barclay. An outstanding and charismatic preacher, it was said that seamen from ships unloading in Bowling Harbour would regularly travel the three miles to Old Kilpatrick just to hear McAulay preach. In 1936, the church was replaced by a new one. One way of raising funds for this appears quite entrepreneurial: reportedly, when the RMS Queen Mary left Clydebank that same year, vantage points were 'sold' to people wishing to view the ship as she made her way down river!

Of the buildings seen here at the top of Ferry Road in this 1920s view, only the whitewashed Canal House has survived. Now a private dwelling house, and externally largely unchanged, it was originally built in the late 1700s to house the bridge keeper. To left of the picture is the railway signal box on the Lanarkshire & Dunbartonshire Railway line. This line was constructed principally to serve the shipyards and engineering works on the north bank of the river. The ticket office and stationmaster's house can be seen to the rear of Canal House, but both, along with the adjacent Gentle's Hall, were destroyed during German bombing in March 1941. The building beyond the signal box housed the offices of Napier & Miller's shipyard. Established in Yoker in 1877, the shipyard moved to Old Kilpatrick when their Yoker site was needed for the new Rothesay Dock. From then, until the closure of the shipyard in 1930, some 123 ships were launched at Old Kilpatrick.

Initially, the old steam-driven ferries (and their later diesel-powered replacements) were able to cope with the vehicular traffic using the crossing on a daily basis. However, by 1948 the increasing number of vehicles was concerning local authorities on both sides of the river. The problem was especially acute during the summer months, when holidaymakers also used the ferries. During such times, the queues of vehicles waiting to board the ferries would line Erskine Ferry Road and often even spill onto Main Street, thereby creating a serious traffic hazard. This problem was finally resolved on 2 July 1971, when Princess Anne opened the newly completed Erskine Bridge. Designed by Freeman Fox and Partners, this towers 140 feet above Old Kilpatrick. The 4,334-feet-long box-stayed girder bridge has a 1,000-feet steel span and, at the time, was the longest non-suspension bridge in Scotland. The last Erskine ferry crossing took place at midnight on the day the bridge was opened.

In May 1906, three red-sandstone tenements were erected to the east of the old Barclay United Free Church, on fields then farmed by James Shanks. Known as the Caledonian Buildings, they were damaged in March 1941 by stray bombs intended for targets in Clydebank. Particularly affected was the nearside corner, occupied here by the Billiards Hall, and painter James Gray. Although the damage was later made good, neither of these two businesses reopened on that site. The latter re-located to Gavinburn Terrace that same year. The business continued to operate until 1969, when James's son, George, retired. Among the other long-established businesses located in Caledonian Buildings were Frank Rennie's upholsterer and furniture repairer, Miss Hay's newsagent's, and William Bruce's confectionery shop. Although Caledonian Buildings remain largely unchanged today, the number of shops on Main Street is now somewhat reduced.

Dalnottar House was built around the 1850s by Charles Stuart, twelfth Lord Blantyre, on the site of an earlier house. Although a substantial building, Dalnottar House was little more than a lodge house for the family as their principal residence was Erskine House, situated on the opposite bank of the river. It has two political claims to fame! Firstly, Lord Blantyre's fourth daughter, Gertrude Stuart, married William Henry Gladstone, the eldest son of Prime Minister, William Ewart Gladstone. Secondly, whilst in the ownership of Sir Robert McAlpine, McAlpine's youngest daughter (who had actually been born in Dalnottar House) married the son of Prime Minister, David Lloyd George. For a period in the mid-1920s and early 1930s, the house was used as a hotel. It was sold to the Ministry of Defence in 1934 and vacated by them in the early 1990s. Despite speculation that it would be redeveloped as a hotel, Dalnottar House was ultimately demolished. Today, new housing stands on the site.

In this 1906 view of Duntocher's Main Street, looking east, the older properties on Bremner's and Filshie's Lands can be seen to the left of the picture. All but the fourth building from the left are now gone and have been replaced with cottages for senior citizens. This surviving property (situated at the corner of Morrison Street) was formerly Filshie's West End Bar, but is now the Village Inn. Further along Main Street (approximately alongside the horse and cart) is Davies Square, where the McGregor family had their long-established grocery. To the right of picture, is the Duntocher West United Free Church and, at the corner of Old Street, James C. Gray's licensed grocery. The church dates from 1822 and was built on ground gifted by the cotton spinning magnate, William Dunn. Its congregation had previously attended Craigs Church in Hardgate but had split on doctrinal grounds, earning them the nickname of the 'new lichts'. Until their new church was built, they had met in the meal loft of a local mill, earning themselves the further nickname of the 'Meal Kirk folk'.

Since at least 1460, when records show that the monks of Paisley Abbey operated a corn mill at Duntocher, the power of the Duntocher Burn has been harnessed to drive such things as waulkmills, an iron works and a spade forge. Its period of greatest importance, however, was in the early 1800s when it powered four large cotton mills. This ruin (seen here around 1910 and nowadays much diminished) is the only remaining visible evidence of these cotton enterprises. This particular mill was situated on the burn near the old Manse Brae. The most complete portion of the ruin is the Engine House and, to the rear of this, can be seen the road leading to Manse Brae. To the right of the photograph are some of the mill workers' buildings, including one known locally as Rooney's House. Also shown is the dam created by the mill falls, in the centre of which is Farrelly's Island. At one time this was the starting point for penny boat trips on the burn.

The Victoria Tomato Farm and Tea Room was opened by consulting engineer, William Young, and his wife, Evelyn, shortly after the completion of the Great Western Boulevard. From here they sold fruit, vegetables and eggs produced on the farm. In addition, they went round nearby villages selling their produce from a horse and cart. To the rear of the farm shop was the tea room, run by Mrs Young. This served a wide selection of cakes, tarts and scones, and delicious ice cream seasonally topped with strawberries grown on the farm. The Tomato Farm and Tea Room was destroyed in 1941 during the Clydebank Blitz. The farm never reopened, but William's son later established a bakery on the site. This was in existence until the early 1950s. Thereafter the site lay derelict for a number of years, before the West Highway Hotel (now the West Park Hotel) was built on it. The fields seen here to the east of the Tomato Farm were laid out in the 1930s for recreational purposes and, later, were used for post-war housing developments.

In 1841, eleven years after Father John Gifford opened a Sunday school at Glenhead, Catholic education in Duntocher was put on a more formal footing when a former Masonic lodge was converted into a chapel-school. This was replaced in 1872 with a new single-storey school in Chapel Road. Comprising only two classrooms, the school's officially designated playground was the road outside the school! Although a second storey was later added, it was ultimately replaced by the school seen here. This new school was a roughcast brick building, with twelve classrooms arranged around a central open quadrangle. Eight of the classrooms were in the west wing, with the other four classrooms, plus the assembly hall, situated in the east wing. The cloakrooms, staffrooms and other non-teaching areas occupied the north and south wings. During the Clydebank Blitz the west wing was completely destroyed and it was not until 1950 that restoration work was completed. Although an extension was built in the early 1970s, and an up-grade carried out in 1998, a new school (opened in 2000) was eventually built on the site.

On 15 August 1873, the local public school serving the Duntocher area was taken over by the then recently formed Old Kilpatrick School Board. A few years later, the original school was replaced with the one shown here. Opened on 8 May 1876, it occupied a site behind Main Street, to the east of Duntiglennan Road and south of Farm Road. It was a primary school, comprising seven classrooms and an assembly hall. It also had a janitor's house (left of the main entrance), and a headmaster's house to the right. The school was completely destroyed by the enemy bombing of 14 March 1941. Thereafter, until other arrangements could be made, pupils were taught in nearby Duntocher West Church Hall. After the war, temporary schooling was provided from hutted accommodation until a replacement school was opened at Goldenhill on 9 September 1955. Today, the site of the school shown in this photograph is occupied by Glenhead Leisure Centre and Library. This was opened in late April 1967 by Matthew Bissett, Chairman of the County Education Committee.

In March 1941 German bombing all but obliterated the several buildings seen here on Roman Road, Duntocher. Among those affected were the old Duntocher Parish Church (later Duntocher Trinity Church) and the buildings on Davie's Haulage Yard, seen here to right of picture. The former, which was opened on 25 September 1896, was built on land gifted by William Dunn. The hall at the rear of the church was added in the late 1890s. For seven years after the Blitz, the congregation worshipped in Duntocher West Church. On 5 September 1948, a new temporary Hall Church was opened, which served the congregation until 10 May 1952 when their new church was opened – the first blitzed church to be rebuilt in Scotland. Unaffected by the bombing was the single-storey cottage to left of picture (known locally as the Sentry House) and the so-called Roman Bridge. Although the latter may at one time have incorporated stones from the nearby Roman fort it is, at best, no earlier than medieval.

The former Hardgate Mill, to the left of the picture on the right, was one of four operated by Kirkintilloch man, William Dunn. Nicknamed the 'King of the Scottish cotton spinning trade', Dunn's first mill was the already-established Duntocher Mill, which he acquired around 1808. This acquisition was followed in 1811 by the Faifley Mill (bought from the Faifley Spinning Company), the Milton Mill (a converted iron works bought in 1821) and, finally, the Hardgate Mill bought in 1831. At their peak, Dunn's mills produced around one million pounds of yarn and two million pounds of cloth each year. The Hardgate Mill, subsequently known as the Hosiery Mill, produced thread and yarn until 1941, when it was badly damaged during the Clydebank Blitz. It never reopened and today the site is occupied by Sammy Kerr's Old Mill Garage. The Duntocher Free Church alongside was established in 1845 by the Rev. William Alexander. It ceased being used as a church in late 1957, and from 1958 onwards it was used as a public hall. Today the building lies derelict.

As early as 1900, proposals were submitted from companies such as the North British Railway and the British Electric Traction Company to either provide a connecting link between Kilbowie Station and Duntocher, or extend the London Electric Power Company tramline from Old Kilpatrick to Duntocher. All these proposals were turned down, and it was not until 1915, when the wooden bascule bridge on Kilbowie Road was replaced with a metal swing bridge, that the Glasgow Corporation tramway service to Dalmuir was extended north, firstly to Radnor Park, and later to Duntocher. Even so, the existence of two low railway bridges meant that only single-deck trams could use this route. These were actually converted ex-Paisley Standard trams, popularly known as 'wee baldies'. With the exception of a few months following the Clydebank Blitz when, due to extensive damage on Kilbowie Hill, the tramway service was curtailed, the trams continued to operate until Saturday, 3 December 1949, when the tram service was withdrawn and replaced with a bus service.

Although today the name Faifley conjures up a modern council estate built in the mid to late 1950s, it was originally a village! In fact, it grew up around the Cochno Road or, as it was formerly known, the Field Road. It was here that early industries, such as waulkmills, iron forges and potteries, were developed, utilising the water from the West and East Burns. On Cochno Road, opposite the Conkrey Dam, was Abraham's Land – named after a Duntocher resident who was head partner in the Union Furniture Company. In this area also, on the locally named Jew's Laun, was Dunn's Faifley Mill. After closure, the mill lay derelict for a period, before being reopened in the early 1900s for the manufacture of furniture. Later it was used by Dairiority for the sale of electrical goods and, from around December 1976 until shortly before demolition in the 1990s, it was a bakery owned by McKechnie's Rolls Limited. The picturesque properties shown here lay on Cochno Road, and no longer stand.

At one time miners' cottages with thatched roofs stood at Hardgate Cross. However, by the turn of the last century, these had been replaced by two-storey properties similar to Victoria Place, seen here to left of picture. Over the years, Victoria Place has been the home of many long-established businesses, such as the flesher, grocer and wine merchant's seen here. From 1926, there was a sweetie shop, run firstly by the Cochrane family and later by Bella Morrison. In 1932 Bella, who also sold groceries, opened a post office facility within the shop. Directly opposite Victoria Place are some of the older tenements on Strang's and Haldane's Lands, and it was here that Tina Donaldson's newspaper shop was located. Within the two-storey building beyond the Cross were the registered offices of the Duntocher & Hardgate Co-operative Society Limited – one of three local co-operative societies. Further east, on the north side of Main Street, is Horn's Wine Bar (later Filshie's Clover Bar). Today, with the exception of Victoria Place (now the Goldenhill Bar), all these buildings have been demolished.

This early view of the junction of Kilbowie Road and Glasgow Road includes the former Craigs United Free Church (to the left of picture). Opened in 1781, this Burgher Secession Church was founded in 1779, when the congregation broke away from the 'mother' church in Old Kilpatrick. For the first two years, services were held in the open air until a small church was built at Craigs. Reputedly, not only was much of the stonework quarried locally by colliers within the congregation, but it is said that the wood and lime used in construction were carried on the backs of the colliers' wives! In 1799, following an ideological dispute, two factions were formed, known as the 'auld lichts' and the 'new lichts'. Thereafter, they embarked on a thirty-year dispute for the right to retain possession of the church. Although the auld lichts were successful, they eventually reunited with the new lichts to form the Craigs & Duntocher United Free Church. The stone wall running across the length of this photograph was known as the 'lazy dyke', reputedly because it was a popular meeting place for local youths, two of whom appear to be doing their best to live up to this nickname!